Hacking

I0004997

The Ultimate Hacking Guide for Beginner's

Introduction

I want to thank you and congratulate you for downloading the book, *"Hacking: The Ultimate Hacking Guide for Beginners"*.

This book contains proven steps and strategies on how to hack computer systems and devices in order to promote better security and ethical computing practices.

This book is all about learning security and preventing malicious networking and physical practices that are designed to steal information or invade privacy. Contrary to popular belief, hacking is not created to promote illegal activities such as these – hacking is actually an ingenious way to thwart these malicious activities.

This book will teach you how to effectively outsmart crackers and script kiddies who are out there to steal your data, or deface a website that you have worked hard for. You will learn the most common infiltration techniques, and learn how to create a strategy to protect yourself by learning how these bad guys of the computing world think and function.

At the end of this book, you will learn how to be a smarter computer and Internet user, and even frustrate people who are trying to access your data without any authority.

Thanks again for downloading this book, I hope you enjoy it!

Chapter 1: What is Hacking?

Hacking, at least according to movies and TV series, is all about gaining access to another computer and taking control over it. If you are interested in this practice, then you might have surface knowledge of what hacking really is. Hacking, in reality, is a wider (and more useful) practice that any person who has a technological device should learn.

Computer Hacking Defined

Hacking, in this book, is the practice of modifying hardware and software in order to make them achieve purposes that their creators might not have thought of when they manufactured it. It is also the practice of making use of loopholes or flaws in a technological design or modules in order to achieve another set of goals other than what the devices are actually and originally made for.

Hack, as a term, was never conceived to be a positive term. If you look at the history of this word, you will realize that it is actually a term for a person who is incompetent at work. A hack was considered to be a cheat made to make people advance through processes in a lazy way. For that reason, some hackers think that this term is actually a poor representation of what they are really capable of doing. After all, hacking is all about being an expert in a particular program or hardware in order to perform advanced, or even undiscovered, uses of technology.

The first hackers existed before the birth of personal computers, and were students at Massachusetts Institute of Technology (MIT). These people created elaborate pranks and jokes at each other, and the designs of their mischiefs are ingenious and very original. After a while, these hacks actually became the predecessor of technological security and computing shortcuts that people know today. While hacking was considered a joke before, it is now a term used to refer to ingenious ways of using a computer.

Are you a Hacker or a Cracker?

Hacking, in the past, only refers to people who are capable of breaking protocols and having wider access to information and purposes of their gadgets, with or without the consent of the manufacturers of any particular hardware or software. Now, the computer technology ensures that there is a wide difference between people who employ ethical practices in hacking; hence, the separation of two types of computer experts: the hacker and the cracker.

A hacker is a person who is more concerned about creating and discovering security protocols in a device. He is also someone who wants to ensure that people maximize the uses of particular software or hardware without breaking the creator's copyright, or access to profit.

A cracker, on the other hand, is more interested in penetrating computer systems in a largely unauthorized way. He creates modifications in a system that may potentially destroy or modify data in order for them to access it, even when he is not supposed to according to the law. He may also be responsible for the distribution of viruses and malwares, or the delivery of spam through computer bots. Because crackers are essentially breaking the law, they are also very knowledgeable in hiding their tracks.

You may consider the knowledge of hacking to be leading you to two potential paths: the Light and the Dark Side, and you can choose to be either Luke Skywalker or Darth Vader. What you will learn in any hacking course can be largely used in order to improve the way you can use technology in such a way that it is supportive to the community that created it, or use it to damage the same people who gave you access to better technology.

At this point, you might want to consider giving hacking and cracking with a grain of salt – real skills are often discovered on how one can protect everyone's rights to access, without having to harm any person's dignity or trade. However, there is no real white and black area in technology anymore. For this reason, this book will teach you a combination of white hat and black hat tricks in order for you to learn the best practices that you can use to maximize computer systems that you may handle on a day-to-day basis.

Identifying your Goals

Your goal is to be an ethical hacker – with that said, you are going to be a master of computer and networking security and provide your computers and online activities the right security audit to ensure that all your data are safe. That means that you learning how to find loopholes and vulnerabilities in your systems should be your main goal. Your second goal should be how to improve your computer system in order to make it more efficient and safe to use.

Also, take note that hacking can take a lot of time and resources when it comes to learning how to hack systems successfully. You need to make sure that you have all the information that you need before you test a hack out on your own system. The reason is simple – you do not want to crash your own PC or website, so make sure that you follow instructions carefully when you are using hack tools or altering computer registries.

Some hacking damages can be irreparable, so make sure that you have backups. If you have a spare PC to test on, then that would be better. Also, remember to stop hacking when a particular goal has been met, such as cracking a passphrase. That will prevent you from crashing your systems to the point that you can't repair them any longer. If you also find a major vulnerability in your system and you are aware that you cannot possibly hack your way into preventing others from exploiting it, then you need to contact a security professional right away. You do not want to be negligent and expose your own system to risks.

Also, remember to keep a log of your practice attacks and resolution times so that you will have an idea regarding how long and how practicable a hacking solution will be when a real-time troubleshooting happens.

Also, keep in mind that hacking tools do not need to be as techie as the ones that you see on television and movies; hacking is a skill that involves great creativity and resourcefulness, and the best hack tools that you can use are the ones that you already have. For that reason, you will discover a great range of tools that are already built in your operating system.

There are also a bunch of tools available for free download from hacking forums and other online communities. As long as you know how to search for the appropriate hacking scenarios and you know what you need to resolve a specific hacking problem, you will find that all that you need are already available.

Chapter 2: Script Kiddy into a Hacker

Here's another thing that you should know before jumping into the world of hacking – hacking involves a lot of work and a great deal of creativity. Without either, you are merely a script kiddy.

Upgrading from Script Kiddy into a Hacker

There are terms that you may encounter in the future when you go to forums. If someone calls you a script kiddy, it means that a hacker or a cracker does not recognize that you have any technical skill when it comes to hacking, and that you do not really know how to create your own programs. Most script kiddies are those who become headlines because they are able to deface unsecure websites; however, they do not really understand how actual programs work.

If you are merely using computer programs without understanding how a computer and its programs really work, but you are highly interested in gaining better access, then it is high time for you to make that necessary upgrade into learning how to actually make things work using what you have.

Getting Started with Hacking

In order to start hacking, you need to learn about these things:

1. Computer Networking

Hacking starts with learning how operating systems work. If you are using a Windows OS, then it is important for you to know how firewalls, network protocols and your favorite programs work.

That means that you have to go beyond the usual usage of a computer. You need to make sure that you are not only able to use Word and surf on the Internet. Your goal now is to learn how to use command lines in Windows, edit your computer's registry to allow or disable particular programs, and tweak with the networking defaults of your computer. You also need to learn how to identify when your computer's security and preferred settings are breached and how to prevent these from happening each time you allow programs to go past the firewall.

2. Available Hack Tools

There are numerous tools out there that will allow you to maximize the utility of your computer and your mobile phone. By observing how these tools work in making computers more efficient, you will be able to discover what direction you want to take as a hacker. You will also have access to these tools for free if you find the right community that share your own hacking goals.

At the same time, it is also high time for you to learn another operating system – Linux. Linux is an OS that most hackers prefer because it allows certain programs to behave beyond what Mac and Windows would allow, such as manipulating processes, texts, and even management protocols in programs. This is also likely to be the OS that you will use when you create your hacking programs.

3. Programming

Programming is the heart of hacking; in order to produce a hack, you need to learn how to write your own codes. Don't worry if you are a newbie when it comes to computers. Programming languages may seem daunting at first, but once you get the hang of how codes work, you will be able to produce a simple hack program. Programming, in an essence, is the ability to communicate to your own computer and the Internet. With this, you can issue commands that will allow you to make full use of available technology.

By learning these things, you get the opportunity to do any or all of the following respectable hacker actions:

1. Solve problems

Hackers are known for being the go-to people when it comes to resolving problems in the computing world. You will discover that they are the ones who create content for all How To websites that allow you to fix even the most complex computer problems, to enabling you to discover content online.

2. Share information

Hackers get reputation by sharing information – be it how to get past YouTube advertisements to speeding up computers. By learning how to do it on your own, you can help other people who want to learn how to improve their experience with their computers.

3. Cooperate with other hackers

Hacking is possible because of a very cooperative community. Without hackers helping one another, open-source programs would not be created and made available for the public to enjoy. By ensuring that everything that you would learn about hacking would also go back to the community, you can contribute to the growth of computer programs that will improve your technological experience as well.

4. Make freedom of information possible

This is where hacking comes into a gray area, but if you believe in unlimited potential of technology, you are also very likely to make actions to make content and technology accessible to people. Hackers dislike secrecy and authoritarian and they believe that people should not be deceived by what others tell them. By creating your own hacks, you will discover that you are capable of providing more people with access to information that will improve their lives.

By knowing how to hack, you will discover how much information is actually available at your fingertips. You will also realize that the information that any tech-savvy individual can help or destroy any organization or personality. As a newbie hacker, you have to take on the responsibility of using the information that the hacking community has already compiled. Arguably, you have to use this information to stop invasion of privacy and unfair maligning of organizations and individuals. To do that, you have to start at the strength of hacking, which is security and discovery of attacks.

Are you ready to be a real hacker? If you are, it is time to review the basics of your available tool: your personal computer.

Chapter 3: Understanding How your Computer and Networking Works

It is a given that you know how to use a computer. However, how well do you understand the way programs and computers work and the reason why they only function up to a limit? In this chapter, you will learn why limits exist when it comes to usage of the computer and why hackers want to upgrade from these limitations, or even exploit them.

Why Computers are Limited

When you first bought your computer, you are probably aware that there is nothing much that you can do aside from installing programs, running them, and then deleting those that you do not use to save memory. These are the options that are available to most computer users.

However, why do computers behave this way? To most hackers, the reasons why options appear to be limited in every computer are the following:

1. **Manufacturers and program creators earn money this way**.

People are mostly interested in making things work right away, and they would be willing to pay or subscribe to offers in order for that to happen. Essentially, this is how hardware and software manufacturers work and earn money. Hackers, on the other hand, want to get the best out of what they had paid up for. You can call this as plainly being a cheapskate, but why buy when you can fix something?

2. **Computers are designed for generic use**.

Most computers are loaded with setting that anyone can make sense of, until their needs become more complex. Most personal computers also enable users to protect themselves from unintentionally destroying their own data, and that happens by hiding the most complex options from users. This also protects companies from getting the blame when something goes wrong with someone's computer.

Computers are often protected by warranty, and it is a mutual agreement between a manufacturer and a buyer. When a buyer agrees to abide by the rules of the warranty, which is not to dissect a computer and use it for purposes that it is not intended for, the manufacturer can give the buyer an assurance that he will get the support that he needs to ensure the safety of his product. Hackers, on the other hand, do not fear the lack of this coverage. With this being said, change how your computer's behavior at your own risk.

Your Computer's Registry

The computer's registry contains the all the information that connect the hardware and software. You can think of this as the part of the operating system that ensures that your computer is running. It is also the part that says what you can and what you cannot do with your computer.

If you are using Windows, you can view and edit a part of the registry using Regedit. It makes the registry readable through text, which of course allows you to manipulate it as well. However, editing it the wrong way can potentially damage your computer, as well as all the data that are stored within it.

If you want to tweak your computer's registry, always remember to back it up first.

Here are some things that you can do with the Windows registry:

1. **Disable windows automatic restart**

Windows Update is probably one of the most useful tools in making sure that your computer is up-to-date, but it is also one of the most annoying ones when it comes to automatically restarting your computer once it is done with its task. It can potentially make you lose data that you are working on when you are not paying attention. You can disable automatic restart and make Windows finish the update when you are not using your PC anymore by pulling up regedit.exe and navigating to

HKEY_LOCAL_MACHINE\SOFTWARE\Policies\Microsoft\Windows\WindowsUpdate\AU

The next step is to create a DWORD value. Name it as NoAutoRebootWithLoggedOnUsers and then assign a value of 1. That will prevent automatic restarts while users are logged on. If you want to put things back, simply delete the value.

2. Enter God Mode to immediately access settings

Control Panel is a neat place to see all the settings on your PC, but it takes forever to navigate it. By enabling the God Mode registry hack, you can place all your settings in one folder in Windows Explorer and display all settings in a single page. You do not actually need to go to regedit to do so, but since it makes use of the Globally Unique Identifiers (GUIDs), it qualifies as an entry in your registry. To create this mode, create a new folder in your desktop and name it as

GOD MODE.{ED7BA470-8E54-465E-825C-99712043E01C}

This will change the icon, and then create a list of all the settings that you need.

3. Take ownership of any file

Ownership permissions are necessary if you need to make changes to a file of folder in your PC. Without it, it might be impossible to run a file the way you want it to. Luckily, a registry hack adds a Take Ownership option into the Context Menu (the menu that appears when you right click a file or folder). To create this option, you need a little help from the hacking community. You can get a file named TakeOwnership.zip, unzip the pack, and then install the TakeOwnership.reg file.

If you do not want to download this file, then you can create the access manually for each file that you want to take ownership of. To do so, do the following:

a. Run Command Prompt as an Administrator,

b. Input takeown /f filepath.

c. Input icacls filepath /grant yourusername:f

Understanding Networking

Networking is the collective term that refers to how a computer can communicate to another device or a group of devices. Since you are getting started on hacking, learning how computer networking works will give you the advantage of gaining access to information over the various connections that are available to your computer. Here are the most important networking terms that you need to keep in mind.

1. **Firewall** – a system that makes use of software, hardware, or both to stop any unauthorized access to a device.

2. **IP address** – refers to Internet Protocol address, which is the fingerprint of any device that connects to a network. It is the address that you can use to identify, track, and locate a device.

3. **Remote Access** – the process that allows a computer's keystrokes and actions to be recognized by another computer as its own, which is similar to how a remote control can manipulate a television. Mostly, it allows data transfer from one computer to another, which also creates access for control

without having to physically manipulate a computer within a specific range. IP addresses are also known as IPv4, which are the common ones that you can find, and IPv6, a newer version that is assigned to newer devices.

4. **MAC address** – or the media access control address. This is the unique ID that every device has and serves as a physical address of all gadgets that you can use to connect to a network. It is usually an address that a manufacturer of a network device assigns to its products.

5. **NAT** – or Network Address Translation. You can use this to share a single IP address to other devices via a router.

6. **DNS** – or domain name system. It allows computers to convert domain names, such as Facebook.com, into an IP address. When your computer contacts the DNS server and it replies back with the numerical IP address of the site that you are trying to log on to, you gain access to the website that you enter on your browser.

7. **DHCP** – or Dynamic Host Configuration Protocol. It allows computers to request an IP address so that you don't have to set up static IP addresses to devices.

8. **Protocols** – These are the ways that a computer communicates over a network. The most common ones are UDP and TCP. A computer switches from one protocol to another, depending on the type of communication that it needs to make.

9. **Packets** – This refers to the unit of data sent between devices on a network. Whenever you log in to a specific website, you are sending packets from your computer, and you receive some of it from another computer. This results to the data that you are able to view on your end.

Judging from the definitions of these terms alone, you get the idea that you are leaving footprints online or on another computer whenever you create an exchange of information. You also get the idea that your computer can be tracked and can be accessed by another computer whenever you do something that grants another computer access. In an ideal world, you can think that this enables anyone to reach you whenever you are in trouble when it comes to using your device.

However, in the world that you live in, networking also allows people to steal information from you and use them for purposes you do not want, prevent you from accessing information that you desire, kick you out of a network, or even render your computer useless. That means that connecting to a network may render positive and negative results, depending on the type of connection that you have and the behavior of people that are also connected on it.

Networking ups the game of computer usage altogether, since it makes it possible for people to make use of data that are not even present in their own devices.

Some Networking Hacks

Here are some of the most common networking hacks that you can use to improve your networking experience.

1. Disable SSID broadcast

Your wireless router has a Service Set Identifier (SSID) that allows it to be searched by computers and connect to it. At the same time, a broadcasted SSID also attracts crackers into potentially considering your Wi-Fi connection as a target. For this reason, it may be wise to consider turning off the SSID broadcast. To do so, log in to your router's GUI, and then turn off the broadcast in the settings.

2. Hide your IP address

Hiding your IP address allows you to use the Internet without leaving any trace of your activity. It also allows you to access websites and online services that restrict certain IP addresses due to their locations. At the same time, it also prevents you from being attacked by crackers who may want to steal your information and track your networking behaviors.

A good way to hide your ID and fool any cracker by displaying a fake IP is to use a Virtual Private Network (VPN). VPNs are great because they do not affect your browsing speed, which allows you to maximize the speed of your Internet connection while concealing your identity. There are numerous reliable VPNs that you can download, such as VyprVPN and Hide My Ass VPN. Alternatively, you can also use website-based proxy servers if you want to remain concealed online without having to download any programs.

3. Check connectivity to another device

If you are getting annoying error messages such as "cannot connect to a remote server", then you may need to see if there are too much networks in another computer that it cannot accommodate your request. You can do so by pinging the IP address or website. If you are using Windows, simply launch Command Prompt and key in ping (name of site or IP address).

Now that you have an idea about the basics, it is time to get into some hacking action.

Chapter 4: Introduction to Digital Forensics

Here is where your knowledge about your computer and the Internet becomes tested: how to track and prevent malicious attacks against your computer. And just like how real crime solving works, in order to catch a thief, you also would sometimes need to think like a thief.

You have the idea that everything that you do will leave digital footprints every time you use a computer. Deleting your surfing history, reformatting your computer, or all your activities online would also not help in concealing information to those who are keen on searching information; there are simply too many ways to find out any information that you have entered in the past online.

Crackers can also recover information that you enter in computers using phishing devices, malware, or entering log files in your computer's registry. However, you can also fight back using the same knowledge that they know, through the use of digital forensics.

What is Digital Forensics?

Digital forensics can be considered as the CSI of the computing world. It is the field that is responsible for determining responsibility for unauthorized digital intrusion and other related crimes. Since attacks against computer security involve a wide range of techniques, digital forensics also involves a wide scope of techniques to identify cybercrime.

Being knowledgeable in digital forensics can help you do the following things:

1. Determine what device or software was used to create and launch a malicious attack

2. Track the source of a malware by finding out its components and signatures

3. Determine when a file was created, modified, or accessed

4. Find out what kinds of sites a perpetrator has visited or the files that he accessed online.

5. Determine who hijacked wireless connections and who are currently using it

6. Recover deleted files, including erased emails

7. Find out the IP and MAC address of the computer that launched the attack and find its location and registered owner

There are many other things that you can do with digital forensics. Now, it is time how to harness these abilities and protect your data.

Open-Source Forensic Suites

If you desire to learn how to track malicious activities in your devices, or find out locations of devices that you interact with, you can use the following tools that are created by the good guys of the hacking community:

1. The Sleuthkit Kit (TSK)

TSK is a collection of Windows and Unix-based tools that allows you to do forensics on computer systems. It can extract data on any Unix, Linux, or Windows computers and find out all the unwanted changes that are done on a computer system. It also allows you to use the Autopsy function, which lets you analyze your hard drives and smartphones and makes it easier for you to find or create custom modules in your devices.

2. Helix

Helix is a live Ubuntu-based CD that is made for computer forensics. It has a special autorun feature on Windows that allows it to take care of forensics and incident responses. It does not mount swap space, or does not automatically mount on any devices that you attach on your PC. Since it is designed to not make any changes on your files and your hardware as much as possible, it is considered to be among the soundest forensics tools.

Some Other Things You Can Do

If you suspect that your computer or network is being hijacked, there are some things that you can do on your end without having to download anything or run any program.

1. Check DNS changes

One of the most common networking attacks that you need to be wary of is DNS hijacking, wherein crackers direct users to another website that is full or advertisements or to a site that looks the same as the intended site in order to steal your login details.

If you suspect that you are a victim of DNS hijacking, check your current DNS settings and see if your DNS is using any of the blacklisted DNS IPs on sites like whatsmyipadress.com. If your IP is listed there, you can change your IP by following your ISPs instructions.

2. Check for malwares and spywares

If you are being prompted by other sites that you have a bad IP address, then you may need to check for malwares in your computer. You can use any trusted anti-virus and anti-malware programs such as AVG. If you suspect that your computer is lodged with key-loggers and other spyware, you would need to use a good spyware removal tool such as Spybot.

Chapter 5: How to Remove Digital Footprints

Every hacker believes that privacy is a right of every individual. However, hackers also know that there are too many ways for Big Brother (and marketing agents too!) to snoop around your activities and possibly even use your devices as surveillance tools. That means to say that most of your activities online and offline are possibly designed to target you for some branding awareness, or probably even put your private life at risk.

What Companies and Crackers Take Advantage Of

If you have a feeling that you are being constantly watched whenever you go online, it is because you probably are. Most websites that you go to make use of your online behavior in order to feed you products that go with the algorithm that prompts the advertisements that you see – something that you can observe whenever you use Facebook. Google is also known for collecting data from its users – just look at the ads that pop up on top of your emails each time you open your mailbox. Of course, you can also count the thousands of spam mails that you receive that clutter your inbox.

On a more serious note, you also expose yourself to risks of being hijacked online when your networking behavior is monitored. Now that you are aware that malwares and phishing tools can be embedded on your devices, it is time to make sure that you prevent feeding crackers and advertisers the very thing that enables them to bug you. It is time to stop leaving data footprints that serve as records of your activities online.

These footprints do not only tell others the sites that you frequently visit, but also RAM usage, downloads, and personal information. Sure, you can make use of the digital forensics tool that you have learned in the previous chapter, but still, prevention is better than cure.

As you already know, communicating with another computer makes it possible for them to know your whereabouts and what your entire life is probably like. If you are into hacking and have goals that may attract people into spying on you, then it is a must that you make sure you manage the following:

1. Cookies

Cookies are small pieces of data that sites store in your hard disk as a text file. These pieces enable websites to remember you as a unique visitor whenever you visit them, and at the same time, do the following:

> a. Allow sites to automatically input your passwords to eliminate the need for you to log-in again

> b. Enable you to have better site experience by storing your preferences during your site visits

> c. Keep track of the items that you select on shopping carts

> d. Record your activities such as browsing history, page visits, click patterns, and interests

Since cookies enable websites to engage you the way you want them to behave, they can also be a threat to privacy. There are sites that may sell cookie data they receive from their users to third party affiliates as leads, which may result into unwanted ads and other popups whenever you visit websites.

2. Personal Information and Passwords

Most users do not think twice about placing their names, email addresses, credit card information, and other sensitive data whenever they are asked to. If you need to enter personal information, then make sure that you are browsing a secure site that does not store this information in order to prevent your accounts from being attacked or spied on.

Now, how do you remove or minimize your footprints to prevent malicious crackers and script kiddies from invading your privacy and stealing your identity? Here are some of the things that you can do:

1. Use private browsing features in browsers, or private browsers

Almost all browsers have private browsing features – Chrome has the Incognito mode, Firefox has the Private Window, and Internet Explorer has the InPrivate Browsing. The private feature prevents your computer from recording your browsing history, and making it seem for those who have physical access to your computer that you have not visited sites that you want to conceal from them.

However, take note that using the Incognito or Private Window would still allow websites to store your data, including your IP address. If you want to browse the Internet more covertly, you can use the application Sandboxie together with private browsing options in your browser to prevent any program from saving data form your disk, including any malwares that may sneak into any online window.

If you want to browse the web as a complete anonymous, you can use the network called Tor. This network's software is proven to prevent any site from recording your IP address. Your ISP will also not record any site that you are visiting. However, Tor comes with a drawback – it is not the fastest browser that you can use, since it makes use of server-bouncing to make sure that your computer remains incognito.

2. Keep private information private

People who have been victims of cracking and network hijacking are likely to be unaware that many of their activities online may tell malicious users that they are just too willing to have their identity stolen. Simply looking at a person's Facebook page would grant access to the most private information about them. It is only a matter of time before crackers and script kiddies use all the information that they can find for identity theft or ransomware, software that steals sensitive information and promises to delete it after a considerable amount of money is received in exchange for data destruction.

The solution can be simple: be sure to check the privacy settings of all your social media posts and make sure that they remain invisible to people who are not your audience. Make sure that you check your Facebook wall and your social media accounts from time to time and change privacy settings of posts that you do not want others to see. If you think that there is still a way for people to recover them, delete them.

3. Search for yourself online

You may be surprised about what you can find out about yourself online when you do a Google search for your name. There is a big chance that you have revealed your private number in your old Friendster account and is now appearing in some obscure site, together with your home address. There is also a chance that you have some racy photos of yourself from a decade ago that can still be viewable via that blog that you wrote when you were still not very knowledgeable about Internet privacy.

If you are able to find information about yourself online, other people can see them as well. Always make sure that you do a clean sweep of your past online activities, especially those that will probably place you at risk. Delete old blogs, unused social networking profiles, and emails that you used to create accounts that you are not using. If you see a content about you that is hosted by someone that you do not know, contact the site's owner or web administrator with a request for its removal. Take note that deleted data may still appear in search engines for some time, but will disappear once these engines update search results.

4. Use a Virtual Private Network (VPN)

A VPN is a type of IP address concealment method that makes your device appear as if it is located in another country, which obscures websites and crackers when it comes to locating you whenever you enter a particular website. In essence, it provides you a virtual location in order to make your Internet usage anonymous. It also makes you access sites that are only available for in-location market, such as some YouTube videos or BBC shows!

The great thing about VPNs is that they are not exclusive for desktop computers – there are numerous VPNs available for smartphones and other mobile devices as well. Make sure that you install VPN apps on all your mobile devices as well so that you can surf the Internet safely while you are on the go.

5. Delete files permanently

If you want to do extra caution, make sure that you delete files permanently and keep your data low. Protection of your files, even the ones on the trash bins, is very important. For this reason, you can use passwords on your personal user account, and for an ounce of extra protection, you can use Bitlocker, a built-in encryption program on newer versions of Windows that encrypts the entire hard drive to prevent access from unauthorized users. If you want the files to be invisible to those who do not have your password, you can use the application called TrueCrypt to hide all your files from other users.

Also keep in mind that deleted files are not totally gone for good – Windows, for example, does not actually remove the data from your drive but simply frees the bits used so that the file system does not point back to them. However, tools like Recuva can recover even the trash emptied by Recycle Bin. If you want to ensure that these files are shredded and gone for good, make use of a program called Eraser to overwrite the data on the drive and ensure that they will never be recovered.

Now that you have learned the basics of concealing yourself from attackers, it is time to test vulnerabilities of your systems by trying to launch attacks.

Chapter 6: Understanding Password Attacks

Password hacking is probably one of the easiest way to attack accounts and computers – most of the time, they are the easiest to guess or retrieve from another person. While everybody knows how to create a strong password, there are just too many people who neglect the responsibility of creating strong passphrases.

The strength of passwords when it comes to protecting computers and networks rely on secrecy – sadly, this is also that one thing that people fail to commit to. When password information is shared to another person, you can trust that accountability goes straight out the window and bad things will start happening. Passwords, then, start to provide a false sense of security to anyone who wants to protect his log-in details.

How Vulnerable is your Password?

Think of one of your passwords and then answer the following questions:

1. Is your password based on something that people commonly know about you, such as the name of your cat, your birthday, or your nickname?

2. Would you think that a friend or someone you know would be able to guess your password?

3. Was the last time you changed your password several months ago?

4. Do you use that password for other accounts as well?

5. Did you write that password in a place where everyone could see?

If you answer yes to most of these questions, then your password could be easily cracked. Time to stop bad password habits and then change your passwords into stronger ones.

Now, these habits are mostly true to most common computer users. Try to guess the password of anyone you know – you would be surprised that most of the traits listed above for a vulnerable password apply to the ones that you can crack. That means that if you are performing as an IT guy and you are supposed to ensure network security in your workplace, most of the people in your office are very likely to leak information out to a cracker!

Ways to Leak Out a Password

How easy is it exactly for a total stranger to crack or obtain a password? Here are the well-oknown ways to get past the log-in page.

1. Social Engineering

Social engineering is a low-tech, yet highly effective, way of getting information from other people. It is the process of conning people into divulging personal information, including passwords. You may think that this is ridiculous, but it is the easiest and most fool-proof way to hack people and gain control of any account.

How to do it:

In order to retrieve a password from a user, all you need to do is practically ask for it. For example, you can call your target anonymously, and say that he has a security breach in his Gmail account. In order to thwart it, he has to provide you his password. If he refuses, ask him to verify his security question and the answer for it.

2. Shoulder surfing

This is another low-tech approach in retrieving passwords and is a common practice in computer shops and public libraries. Simply put, shoulder surfing is watching someone key in his log-in details.

How to do it:

Do a random testing in a place where people normally log in into their computers, preferably your workplace or at home where your housemates would normally use computers or smartphones. Try to not look obvious and look at their keyboards or screens when they attempt to enter their log-in details. If you didn't see the password, you can make a guess according to their keystrokes – all you need to do is make out possible words at the area of the keyboard where they are typing.

3. Use password-cracking software

If it is not possible to crack a password by inference or by asking for it, then it is time to progress into doing high-tech measures. Take note that these measures are actually harder to employ, but can generate very useful results to any hacker.

There are numerous applications out there that can crack password combinations. Here are some of the most popular password cracking tools:

a. Proactive System Password Recovery – can recover any stored Windows, WPA/WEP, VPN, or SYSKEY passwords

b. Elcomsoft System Recovery – cracks Microsoft Office, PKCS, and PGP passwords. Great for opening documents that are password-protected

c. Proactive Password Auditor – uses a combination of techniques, including brute-force, dictionary, or rainbow technique to extract passwords

d. RainbowCrack – cracks MD5 and LanManager passwords at a great speed.

e. John the Ripper = cracks Linux, Unix, and Windows passwords

Take note that most password cracking tools may require physical access to the device that you are cracking. Now, it brings forward another security threat – a physical computer has more personal information than an online account that has been breached. If you think that your personal computer can easily be physically accessed and then be cracked open with these tools, then you need to employ better security.

4. Keystroke logging

A keystroke logger can be software or hardware that can be installed on a computer or device to record keystrokes whenever a log-in action takes place. Take note that this technique is highly illegal, so be cautious when testing it out on any computer.

How to do it:

You can download keylogging applications such as SpectorPro, eBlaster, or Keylogger Stealth. If you want to do physical logging, then you can get the hardware KeyGhost to fit between the keyboard and the device, or replace the keyboard altogether. Take note that keylogging software can be traced by any decent spyware detection application and keyboard logging devices can also be detected with a keen eye.

As a countermeasure, always see to it that you check keyboard devices whenever you use a public computer. If you see an additional attachment in between the computer and a keyboard that looks like a USB connector, then try to remove it and see if the keyboard still works. If it does, that connector is most likely a keylogging device.

5. Search for password storage

This technique makes use of another human vulnerability – the inability to remember passwords.

How to do it:

It normally takes a simple text search in computer systems – all you need to do is to search using the Windows search function, or make use of grep or findstr search in the command prompt. Try to search for the words password or passwd on the local drives and you would discover system files that actually log passwords for numerous applications.

Chapter 7: Network Hacking

Network infrastructures refer to any cracker and script kiddie's hijacking dream – not only would a hijacked network allow them to post on a website about any content that they can think about, it also allows them to get total control of any software and hardware in the network. Remember remote desktop assistance? The ability to tap that access in a network that connects multiple computers serves as an instant gold mine.

The good news about network infrastructures is that vulnerabilities can easily be discovered and eliminated by simply upgrading firmware and patching network hosts – something that most third party network security offices would do for any client company that they handle. As long as all the computer users in your vicinity are vigilant when it comes to accessing their computers and you see to it that you do a spyware and malware sweep religiously, you technically have almost nothing to worry about when your computers are attacked from the outside. These attacks would only be able to scratch the surface, and would not be as detrimental as you think.

Where Networks are Most Vulnerable

When looking at your computer's network infrastructure, you need to check for the following:

1. How firewalls and IPS are configured and located

2. What crackers normally see when they perform port scans

3. Your network's design, which comprises of Internet connections, remote access abilities, defenses, and hosts

4. Commonly attacked ports that are still unprotected

5. Configurations of network hosts

6. Network maintenance and monitoring

All of these things comprise the security of a network. Once any of these factors are compromised, you will most likely face the following problems:

1. A Denial of Service (DoS) or Distributed Denial of Service (DDoS) attack, which is designed to take down all network connections, including your Internet connection. In a DoS or DDoS attack, the attacker attempts to flood your system with tons of useless information to overload your network. It is hard to detect as computers process the incoming traffic as normal activity. The only way to prevent it is to detect the bad IP address where the traffic is coming using a computer that is not attached to the network.

2. Use of network analyzer which serves as a tool to steal sensitive data from emails and local files

3. Host attacks on unprotected local vulnerabilities

4. Backdoor setups that may allow crackers from stealthily infiltrating your system without sounding alarms

5. Steal information through DNS hijacking from everyone that uses your network

Without proper testing of vulnerabilities, the range of trouble a computer system can get is undeniably wide. You can lose all your important data and also allow someone to render your computer network worthless in a single successful attack. For this reason, you need to do the following

1. Map your network.

2. Scan your networking systems and see which are working.

3. Determine which processes are running on working systems.

4. Attempt to penetrate the working system to check if defenses are up.

How to Test for Vulnerabilities

Luckily, there are several tools that the hacking community has provided to check for security loopholes. There are some of the tools that you can use:

1. GFI LANGuard – used for scanning ports and testing vulnerabilities

2. Nessus – all-in-one tool for ping sweeps and port scanning

3. NetScan Tools Pro – great commercial tool for gathering network data, such as active IPs, MAC addresses, and NetBIOS in your system. It also allows you to fingerprint all the OS attached to different hosts.

Using these tools, or other similar ones available in the market, will help you uncover the following cracking practices that are used to map out a network system to plan an attack:

1. **Port Scans**

This is the most common type of network probe. A port scan allows any cracker to poke through the network and see all the services that are running on a machine that they are targeting. It also allows them to see what kind of security is available and what kind of vulnerabilities are available.

For example, if a cracker takes note that port 143 is open and she figured that the IMAP on that port is crackable, then he knows he would be able to worm through that port by using an exploit. An exploit is a term for any program that takes advantage of security holes. It can be a Trojan horse or a malware, depending on the takeover goal that the cracker has.

Port scans are very easy to do. All you need to do is to connect to ports and find out which ports are responding and which ones are not. If you know how to code in Java or Perl, then you can write a port scan program in under 15 minutes.

However, numerous anti-spying devices can easily detect port scans. If a computer detects that there is a single device that tries to poke on different ports at the same time or within short intervals, then the computer will alert the user that a possible attack is taking place.

2. **Ping Sweeps**

A ping sweep is a kind of network probe that allows the intruder to send a bunch of ICMP ENHO packets to a network, usually by specifying a bunch of IP addresses. Similar to a port scan, a ping sweep determines which machines are responding and which are not. Once the intruder is aware that the devices that he "knocked on" are alive, then he could plan his attack.

Take note that attacks are getting more sophisticated, and if you suspect that your computer network is being probed by an attacker, they have already anticipated that your next move is to identify their machines and also trace their locations. At this point, the attacker knows that he has to do the probe using a VPN to become anonymous. So what's your move now? You have to concentrate on your goal and make sure that you patch your ports to prevent a possible hijack.

Protect Your Internet Connection

In a previous chapter, you have the idea that disabling the SSID broadcast in your Wi-Fi can prevent attackers from targeting your connection and having access to the network of computers that are attached to it. Disabling the broadcast can also make it harder for an attacker to know that you are just within range and simply become persuaded to turning their attention to someone else. That can be a start move, unless the attacker already knows your SSID and the address of your Wi-Fi.

The solution for this is to restrict the MAC addresses of devices that can connect to your Wi-Fi. You can easily do that by changing the settings on the GUI of your Wi-Fi adapter, and then manually inputting all the MAC addresses of all the devices that you would allow to connect to your Wi-Fi. However, attackers have a workaround for this, which is called MAC-spoofing.

MAC-spoofing is a tried and tested method in getting more Internet hours in a public hotspot location such as cafes and airports, and also probe into a MAC-protected Wi-Fi for access. Attackers can use a WLAN Analyzer to look for a target and see all the MAC addresses that it allows to connect, and simply spoof their MAC address to match one of the allowed ones. Afterwards, they can request for an IP address by inputting ipconfig/renew on the command prompt. To test if it is working, they can ping a web address or simply load their favorite website.

To prevent this from happening, always make sure that you add an extra ounce of protection by enabling a WPA2 password. If you suspect that that is cracked, you can invest in enabling wireless IPS. That costs money, but it adds an extra layer of protection that is harder to crack.

When you think about protecting your network from crackers, take note that vigilance and good computer usage habits will actually prevent most of the attacks launched on computers nowadays. By seeing to it that your network infrastructures are also well-maintained and checked for vulnerabilities, it will be easier to persuade crackers to leave your network alone.

Conclusion

Thank you again for downloading this book!

I hope this book was able to help you to uncover cracking practices and make use of tools that will thwart any opportunity to hijack your system. I also hope that this book has helped you discover vulnerabilities in your computer and make you observe better security when it comes to protecting your files and logging in to any website that you visit.

The next step is to make sure that you perform routine maintenance by launching test attacks on your systems to achieve security goals. Make sure that you exercise good caution in testing these vulnerabilities to maintain the integrity of your system.

Finally, if you enjoyed this book, then I'd like to ask you for a favor, would you be kind enough to leave a review for this book on Amazon? It'd be greatly appreciated!

Thank you and good luck!

Preview of my other books that might interest you:

HTML: Step by Step Beginners Guide to HTML

The book *"HTML: Step by Step Beginners Guide to HTML"* will provide all essential information and training during the book which you'll need in order to upgrade your skills later with other languages and even with more sophisticated HTML.

The reason why we start our *"Learn Web Design"* series with HTML is because he is the core to every website out there. No matter how basic or sophisticated one website is the HTML is always there and is essential for its existence.

In order to perfectly understand the material we'll go through everything from the absolute beginning. We'll do some exercises because the only way to master programming is by constant exercise and learning.

All the material in this book can be learned in less than a day but exercising and upgrading your skills later on is essential to becoming a good programmer.

You can check/download the book from <u>HERE</u>.

Java
Learn Java Programming with the Ultimate Crash Course for Beginners in no Time!

Today's applications are becoming increasingly powerful, especially with computers, smartphones, and tablets getting more processing power and memory every year. However, all of these devices are nothing without the operating system and programs they contain.

You might already be familiar with Java, whether it's from an introductory course in programming or a platform you had to install to make certain programs work on your computer, and that's not surprising at all since Java remains one of the most popular and in-demand programming languages in the world!

Despite the popularity of Java as a language and a platform, there remains still a shortage of qualified programmers to create meaningful and useful Java applications. Whether you're completely new to Java, or even to programming, or you feel that there's still a lot of room for improvement in terms of your current Java programming skills, this book will give you a strong foundation in both programming and Java.

If you're still wondering whether or not this book is for you, here are some statements to help you decide:

- You're a complete newbie and you need a book that introduces you gently to the world of programming
- You're already a Java developer but you'd like to sharpen your skills and create more efficient, error-free code
- You want to find a book that isn't overly technical but at the same time, not too dumbed-down
- You enjoy solving riddles and challenges
- You have a really good idea for a program and nobody has thought about it just yet
- You want to help people by creating programs that they need but can't seem to find

If you can identify with any of these statements, then you've come to the right place. This book provides a self-paced comprehensive crash course in Java, from the very definition of programming to the most advanced topics in Java. This book will provide plenty of source codes for you to play and experiment with in order to help you understand Java better. After finishing this book, you should be able to create Java programs confidently.

This book can serve as both a reference and a walkthrough in Java, so feel free to skip and skim through chapters that talk about things you're already well acquainted with and jump back and forth between chapters if that works better for you.

C
Learn C # Programming with the Ultimate Crash Course for Beginners in no Time!

This book contains proven steps and strategies on how to start writing programs with C# in the soonest time possible!

If you have prior knowledge about the world of *C++* programming, then you may find familiar terms and code structure with *C#* (pronounced as *See Sharp*). It works with Microsoft *.NET* framework and was initially designed to be the answer to *Java*. Today, both are being used extensively by companies and are also a friendly language for beginners.

Here are some of the essential lessons you will find inside:

- *Comprehending the C# Program Structure*

- *The Coding Conventions for C#*

- *Mastering Variables and Data Types*

- *Getting Using Input and Using Type Conversions*

- *Arithmetic, Conditional, Relational, and Logical Operators*

- *Using Flow Control Statements*

- *Generating Random Numbers*

- *And much more!*

You can check/download the book from HERE.

HTML5 & CSS3

Learn HTML5 and CSS3 in One Day with Hands-on project and learn them Well!

This book contains proven steps and strategies on how to design projects using HTML5 and CSS3.

It's not only hardware that is evolving. The software that makes our hardware tick has also evolved by leaps and bounds. And the programmed processes that these software undertake have even shared in this progress.

This book will teach you about the most important aspects of two of the Internet's next-gen technologies -- HTML5 and CSS3. These systems will be running in each and every cutting-edge site, web app, or mobile application in the very near future -- in fact, many have adapted it even now. Read on to be on the forefront of the Internet's next frontier!

<u>You can check/download the book from HERE.</u>

PHP & MySQL
Learn PHP and MySQL with the Ultimate Crash Course for Beginner's In No Time!

This book contains proven steps and strategies on how to create codes using the correct syntax, keywords, and punctuation marks. It also provides tips on how to correctly use arrays and conditional statements. There are sample programs that can serve as your guidelines when writing your code.

This book also contains useful information about MySQL and PHP, including their histories and features. It even discusses the differences between MySQL and PostgreSQL

You can check/download the book from HERE.